WomWom is in her burrow.
There is dung around the
burrow.

Dung is a way WomWom removes waste from her body. WomWom makes dung. The dung goes on to the soil. Dung is food for plants.

When WomWom goes for a
walk on the beach she sees
rubbish. She does not know
what to do with this rubbish.
This rubbish does not help
plants or animals grow.

Where should this plastic
bottle go? It does not belong
on the beach. WomWom
sees the rubbish bin.

WomWom smells the rubbish. It does not smell like food. Should WomWom eat it?

No WomWom! Don't eat rubbish! Animals can get sick if they eat rubbish.

WomWom eats grasses and
plants to be healthy. Visitors
to the farm do not leave
rubbish.
Rubbish could make
WomWom sick.

Rubbish dropped in the sea can wash up on the beach. The rubbish can make birds and animals sick. Farmer Addy and WomWom pick up rubbish.

How can we help keep
animals safe? We should
remove all rubbish. This will
help keep animals safe.

Farmer Addy and WomWom
collect glass bottles. The
bottles will be reused again.
Farmer Addy recycles the
glass from bottles.

There is no rubbish on the farm. The plants are fresh and clean. WomWom loves to eat the fresh and clean plants.

When WomWom gets tired she goes to her burrow. There is no rubbish in her burrow. We can help protect WomWom. We should keep her world safe and clean.